Adam Hopkins/Gaby Macphedran

Law and Order

Macdonald

A MACDONALD BOOK

First published in 1985 by
Macdonald & Co. (Publishers) Ltd
London and Sydney

Reprinted 1987

© Adam Hopkins/Gaby Macphedran 1985

ISBN 0 356 10320 X

Macdonald & Co. (Publishers) Ltd
Greater London House
Hampstead Road
London
NW1 7QX

A BPCC plc company

Printed in Great Britain by
Purnell Book Production Ltd
Member of the BPCC Group

BRITISH LIBRARY
CATALOGUING IN PUBLICATION DATA

Hopkins, Adam
    Law and order.—(Debates)
    1. Law—England   2. Youth—Legal status,
    laws, etc.—England
    I. Title   II. Macphedran, Gaby   III. Series
    344.2′0024055   KD665.Y6

    ISBN 0-356-10320-X

Contents

Do we need

All people who live in social groups develop some rules of behaviour which govern the way they live. In the simplest social unit, there are accepted codes concerning how men and women live together, how they rear their children, gather their food and protect themselves. The survival of the community depends on its members accepting these rules as being for the common good.

As our social organizations become more complex, so do the laws which govern our lives. The collective responsibility of the small group gives way to a system of law imposed from above.

Human nature? There is a tradition of philosophical thought which holds that people are by nature evil and corrupt. Left to themselves, they will live their lives in a state of disorder and violence, where might is right and terror reigns. It is only the force of law and the presence of government which make them suppress their baser instincts and behave in a socially acceptable way. As Thomas Hobbes described it, a life unrestrained by authority would be 'nasty, brutish, and short'.

> '*Where there is no law, there is no freedom.'*
> *John Locke*, Treatise of Government, *1690*

The opposite view was held by Jean-Jacques Rousseau, the French philosopher. He saw man as 'the noble savage'. People are born in innocence, free and unrestrained, Rousseau argued, and their natural preference for co-operation and order will prevail. It is their social environment and the laws imposed on them that corrupt.

Anarchists have inherited this view. For

law?

them a just society cannot be achieved by the imposition of laws. These merely create oppression and tyranny. Government destroys freedom. The abolition of private property will eliminate greed. Education and voluntary co-operation will make the state and its laws unnecessary.

The individual or the state? The aims behind the legal system in the West take into account the views of both Hobbes and Rousseau. The idea is that individuals should be left as free as possible to determine the conditions of their own lives as long as by doing so they do not impinge on the rights of others. In theory, there is an independent legal system to maintain these rights, if necessary against the state itself. Law is seen as necessary, to protect the freedom of the individual.

From the Marxist point of view, however, there can be no just legal system in a capitalist society because the ruling class will always use the law to protect its own interests. But in conditions of true Communism the state and its legal apparatus will 'wither away'. There will be no need for penal laws where there is no class conflict and where the will of the people is expressed in the leadership of the Communist party.

But in trying to achieve these ideal conditions, Communist countries rely on the centralized machinery of the state and the heavy force of law. Communist leaders accept this as an inevitable but temporary state of affairs.

Left Society works in complicated ways to supply its own needs. Behind this peaceful market scene lies the complex cooperation of many people. Would the system work without rules and regulations?

'Man is born free; yet everywhere he is in chains.' Jean-Jacques Rousseau, The Social Contract, 1762

Whose law?

Most governments claim that the laws which rule their society operate in the interests of the people as a whole. This is true of régimes of the left and right, both totalitarian and democratic. However, some of their citizens, perhaps large numbers of them, would not agree with their claim.

Misuse of law? South Africa is frequently criticised for its one-sided attitude to law. It operates a system of apartheid – or 'separate development of the races', as the government prefers to call it. There are 21 million black Africans compared to four and a half million whites, yet whites receive three-quarters of the national income. The black Africans are restricted to the so-called Bantu homelands – the poorest 13.7 per cent of total land space. But there is no work. For this, they have to come into white South Africa, where they have no say at all in public life.

Protests against racial injustice in South Africa often lead to prosecution in the courts under the Suppression of Communism Act, even though most of them have little connection with Communism. However, at Sharpeville in 1960, police opened fire on a protesting crowd. At Soweto in 1976, 100 died and 1,000 were injured. Nevertheless, the government claims to be governing in the interests of all the people.

The Communist countries, too, come in for criticism for their attitude to the law. In Russia it is clear that there are groups of people who feel the laws of the land do not reflect their interests. Minority religious groups claim they are being persecuted for their beliefs. In Poland, the 'Solidarity' movement for free trades unions enjoyed widespread support. But in the end it was firmly suppressed by the government in the name of law and order. Whose law? And whose order?

Scene in a South African township. Riot police use specially trained German shepherd dogs to keep an angry crowd under control. But very often such confrontation ends with the death of Africans.

'The law in its majesty shows neither fear nor favour.'
Appeal Court judge, 1895

Whose order?

The governments of these countries can be described to some degree as 'totalitarian' – a system where all aspects of daily life are under the control of one party and where opposition is not tolerated. But many people say that the democratic freedoms of the West are equally an illusion.

By mandate of the people? In the West, liberal democratic governments generally argue that their legal system reflects the consensus of opinion among the population, the customary beliefs and traditional values of decent, honourable citizens. Each time a new government is elected, its justification for changing laws and making new ones is supposed to spring from 'the mandate of the people'. But what do Western governments really mean by 'the people'?

Governments in power are naturally interested in remaining in office, so they have to retain the popular vote that got them elected. To do this they sometimes act in the interests of the majority in ways which may seriously damage minorities.

In recent years both the American and British governments have been accused of acting against the interests of trades unions and working people in favour of big business. Some people feel that the rights of the Aborigines have not been properly protected in Australia. And when the minority Tamil population in Sri Lanka have tried to reassert their own rights, they have met violent repression at the hands of the army and the government.

> 'Law is in almost every country the favourer of the rich against the poor.'
> William Godwin, philosopher, 1798

The labour organization Solidarity was outlawed by the Polish government. Even so, crowds held its banner high during the visit of Pope John Paul II in 1983.

Is public order

Many people believe we are living through a period of unprecedented growth in crime, particularly street crime, violence and disorder. Deep feelings of fear and indignation are commonly expressed. But it must be remembered that a great many people have held the same belief throughout history. Is it really happening this time?

A soaring crime rate? A scrutiny of the crime figures in every industrialized country except Japan seems to show a truly staggering increase in the amount of recorded crime. Some experts state roundly that the amount of serious crime has quadrupled in the past 25 years. Ninety-five per cent of recorded crimes are against property. The proportion of violent crime such as murder, robbery with violence, rape and other sexual offences has remained constant at about five per cent. But as the total number of recorded crimes increases, so too does the number of violent offences.

> *'We see a future where policemen are murdered and the public are afraid.'*
> *Chairman of the Police Federation, 1975*

The growth in the amount of crime has been accompanied by a sharp drop in the rate of detection and conviction, known as the clear-up rate. It is the combination of rising crime and falling clear-up rate that provokes fear.

What is more, studies of the victims of crime show that many crimes go unreported. This means there is a 'dark figure' for crime on top of government statistics.

But are the figures true? Experts have pointed out repeatedly that the recorded figures for crime are not 'facts' in the ordinary sense of the word. It all depends on what you mean when you label a particular crime. What is a criminal assault, for instance, and what is just an ordinary fight to be forgotten as quickly as possible?

There is evidence to suggest that one reason why crime appears to be rising is a decrease in public tolerance of violence, even in areas where violence was once commonplace. This means that people are far more likely to bring it to the attention of the police.

There are practical reasons, too, for the increased reporting of crime. Today all car thefts are reported to the police. This is

breaking down?

because all cars have, by law, to be insured. Their owners naturally wish to claim the value of the stolen car on insurance but cannot do so unless they have told the police. More and more burglaries of household goods are reported for the same reason.

Another problem involves the use of police resources. If the police are concentrating their attention on a particular kind of violent behaviour, then they will probably deploy larger numbers of officers than usual in areas they consider to be at risk. The figures for that offence will then begin to rise quickly – which they would not have done without the extra police being deployed.

These and other problems lead many who have made a serious study of crime to express grave doubts about the figures.

'The average person can expect a robbery once every five centuries.' Official statistic, 1983

Japanese students, in white helmets, armed themselves as if for war when police tried to break up their demonstrations against a new airport in Tokyo, 1969. Nothing like this had been seen before.

Rich crime,

There are two main strands to the law and order argument. One side calls for tough policing, longer prison sentences and often for the use of the death penalty. This group concentrates on crimes of violence, particularly attacks on the police, the elderly and the helpless; theft of personal property in general and 'mugging' in particular; 'scrounging' on social security; drug abuse; and on other wider aspects of behaviour that it finds unacceptable, such as sexual immorality. These are matters that produce intense fear and moral disapproval among a large section of the population.

A completely different point of view, however, concentrates on more 'respectable' activities like tax evasion, fraud, embezzlement, computer crime, 'fiddling' at work, and dangerous breaches of safety regulations to increase company profits. Though it may be said that all of these are extremely damaging, they normally generate less heat in argument. They are often called 'white-collar crimes'.

Are young people to blame? It is a widely held view among traditional law and order supporters that young people are responsible for a great many of the crimes which provoke outrage. The figures at first sight support this view. In Britain, for example, the official publication *Social Trends* shows a large overall increase in the number of serious offences by people of 20 or under between 1961 and 1982.

The figures for individual crimes show young people leading the way in all forms of theft and burglary and in causing criminal damage (this includes vandalism). But the majority of crimes of direct personal violence are committed by people over the age of 21.

Self-report surveys – that is to say, studies where people tell about their own actions – suggest that most young people do something criminal at some time or other, most typically stealing. But history shows that this has been equally true in the past, so that it may simply be part of the process of growing up.

Early morning business commuters on their way to work. They look respectable – but how law-abiding are they?

'Most of the "criminals" do not regard what they are doing as remotely blameworthy.'
Gerald Mars, anthropologist

poor crime?

The acceptable face of crime? There is little public fuss about white-collar crime. Tax evasion in particular is universally condoned (the 'get away with what you can' attitude). In some circles it is almost a game, despite the fact that it costs the state, and therefore all other tax-paying citizens, enormous sums of money.

White-collar crime in total is extremely expensive. In the USA, for instance, it costs three times as much as 'traditional' crimes against property. This proportion is likely to increase if the present growth in computer crime continues.

One reason for the lack of public concern is that the costs of such crimes are spread invisibly among great numbers of people. One public company lowered its costs by adulterating the ingredients of a fruit drink. It continued to charge the old price, so everybody who drank the drink was deceived into paying a tiny fraction more. This was no great loss to any individual but a huge illegal gain to the company. So only the law enforcement agencies were worried.

Another reason is that crimes committed by rich people often attract less attention in the media than the crimes of the poor. This may be seen in the differing treatment of tax evaders and those who make false claims on social security.

Young people are highly visible, especially when they hang around in groups with nothing obvious to do. Police and other adults often treat them with suspicion.

'Don't work –
rob the rich.'
Street slogan

Why do

There has been little research into the causes of white-collar crime. The reasons for crimes of violence, street crime and theft, however, are the subject of fierce argument.

Criminals are born, not made? This point of view has its origins mainly in the religious idea that human beings are born sinful. They commit crimes because their nature is depraved and selfish and they will continue to do so until they come to love God more than they love themselves.

A similar view says that people commit crimes because they are born with a moral or physical defect. It was once believed there was a criminal appearance – with low forehead and a violent, threatening look – and that this was associated with 'feeble-mindedness'. Testing in American prisons after the First World War (1914-18) indicated that criminals were no more feeble-minded than society at large; but some people still cling to the old belief.

Many crimes are associated with alcohol, and drinking was once considered a character defect, probably inherited. But when the serious study of crime began, people started to realize that crime was increasing roughly in proportion to society's increased consumption of alcohol. Drinking had become relatively cheaper and more acceptable socially. So it was a change in social factors, not morals, that led to an increase in the consumption of alcohol and the related rise in crime.

Society makes criminals? A widely held modern view is that the main cause of crime is the pressure of circumstances acting on the individual. Poverty and a deprived environment are often taken as the most important factors of all. The whole idea is provocative to law and order advocates because it suggests that criminals cannot be held responsible for their actions and should be more pitied than blamed. This theory runs into trouble, however, because many people who are poor are also totally honest.

The extreme version of the 'social' view is that criminals are reacting against society's injustice and that they are right to do so. The more criminals there are, the more the ruling class is under attack and the sooner the revolution will come.

Groups under pressure? Research in Chicago into the arrival of successive waves of immigrants into the city showed that each wave in its turn was unruly and often criminal until the new arrivals were settled and

> ## 'She had nothing for Christmas so I took it.'
> *Mother convicted of shoplifting, 1984*

Opposite If your life is desperate, are you more likely to turn to crime? Conditions are bleak for many in the decayed industrial cities of the old world and the shanty towns of the new.

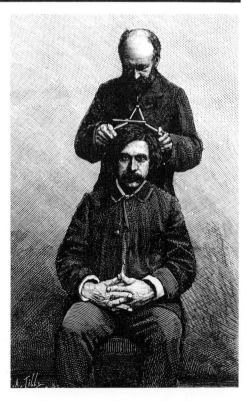

A nineteenth-century French criminal is having his head measured. Scientists were investigating the theory that criminals had special physical characteristics.

they do it?

prosperous. There was nothing special about the individual groups or races to make them criminal. What mattered was the experience of the group as a whole and, as its experiences changed, so did its behaviour.

The same thing is happening today. In Britain, for example, through poverty, lack of jobs and general loss of opportunity because of their colour, there is special pressure on young black people of Caribbean origin.

They are blamed for a disproportionate number of street crimes. The 'group' point of view accepts this as realistic but says it has nothing to do with race and will not continue when circumstances change.

> *'No way I'd take a job. This is my job.'*
> Professional burglar

The victims –

Elderly people are vulnerable. Even so, most live out their lives without suffering directly from the effects of crime.

The law and order campaign gains much of its strength from the popular belief that devastating crime may strike out suddenly at any one of us. Elderly people, hearing of atrocious acts committed against people like themselves, lock their doors and stay at home. But how soundly based is their fear?

The muggers can get you anywhere? Statistically American cities are the most dangerous in any developed country. Yet a recent survey showed that in Britain, where the crime rate is far lower, the level of fear was 15 per cent higher. How this can happen has been studied very closely in the case of mugging, the offence

'Look, mate, who's got the money? A granny? Or a young bloke on pay day?'
Youth on probation

who are they?

which has caused most alarm. And much of the blame appears to lie with newspapers.

The term 'mugging' originated in the USA where it was associated with inner city ghettoes and racial violence. Newspapers began to use the word frequently in the early 1970s and it has since become commonplace, reinforced by occasional police statistics which accuse young blacks of a disproportionate involvement. But researchers say that in London, for example, mugging represents less than one per cent of serious crime. It happens almost entirely in the poorer areas where most young blacks live. Most of the victims of attack by black youths are themselves young and male, and a sizable proportion are black.

According to researchers, attacks on old people are in fact unusual and achieve press prominence for this reason. But they are presented as if they were typical. When an issue like mugging gets disproportionate and emotive attention from press and public, this is called a 'moral panic'.

Because some researchers openly disapprove of the authoritarian attitudes of law and order campaigners, their findings are often received with scepticism by those who feel they deliberately minimize crime.

Who suffers most? Law and order advocates see crime as widespread in society, with the old and helpless particularly at risk. Official figures, however, indicate that those most likely to suffer assaults in fact are male, under 30 years of age, single, widowers or divorced, spend several nights a week out, drink heavily and themselves assault others.

In the USA those who are poor, young and black are far the most likely to suffer from attack. Overall more people die in motor accidents than through violence yet, according to the 1980 Statistical Abstract, more black people per 100,000 die by homicide than white people die in car accidents. Few white women die violently but black women are actually more likely to be killed than white men. These statistics underline the close relationship between comparative poverty and being a victim of crime.

Fear of crime is greatest among those least likely to suffer – women and the elderly. This has led some people to argue that they should try to worry less. A more sympathetic attitude is to accept that violence against the old and crimes of sexual violence like rape are truly to be feared, whatever the statistics. Moreover, crime is so frequent in some inner city areas that women and elderly people living there are statistically justified in their fear.

It is certainly clear that those who need most protection are the poorest and the weakest, whatever their age, sex or race.

> *'They knocked me down and kicked me in the head – for a handful of coins.'*
> *Pensioner, 1984*

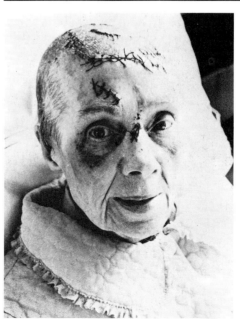

This woman was attacked by burglars in her own home. Her experience is of the kind which makes almost all old people feel afraid.

The trouble

W hen people speak of the need for law and order, they often conjure up an image of youths who are unruly and disrespectful, whether or not they have actually committed any offence. It is said that the family structure has broken down, that schools exert no authority and that the church has lost its power. Young people have set aside the normal decencies and become a threat to the stability and comfort of society.

Is this really true, as law and order advocates believe, or is it a matter of appearances? If it is the latter, how much does appearance matter?

How bad is bad behaviour? Violence related to sport has become a particular problem. Football hooligans have invaded pitches, vandalized railway carriages, attacked spectators from opposing teams, and terrified members of the public. This behaviour has been exported when home teams play abroad.

Other current charges against young people are in part to do with style. From the Teds and Beatniks of the '50s and the Flower Power people of the '60s, by way of Mods and Rockers to Skinheads, Punks and Rastafarians, young people have asserted a lifestyle that shocks the more established and settled members of the community. Many of these styles have been associated in the public mind with drugs and violence.

To law and order supporters, all these forms of behaviour are almost uniformly bad. Football hooligans are described as 'primitive', 'animal' or 'mindless'. In other cases, the very style adopted by the young is taken as evidence of deviance which is by definition a threat to civilized society.

Is there a message? Some experts, however, believe that these forms of behaviour should be understood before they are condemned. Far from being 'mindless', it could be argued that many of them, and perhaps even football hooliganism, carry a message for society – one of boredom and disillusion.

This argument stems from the premise that orthodox society – that is to say, respectable, law-abiding citizens – establish their own way of behaving and try to make other people behave in the same way. When particular groups of youths genuinely disagree with the values of the older generation, they express their disagreement by adopting their own style.

In truth, young Skinheads in huge boots or Rastafarians in a group on a street corner are challenging the existing order at a certain level. But is repression the answer? Should society not perhaps try to meet the needs they feel?

What about the violence? Many of our images of unruly behaviour come from the media. Some say the press are in large part

Football hooliganism in Latin America. Police clear the stands with tear gas.

with kids?

responsible for the violence. It has been clearly shown, for example, that the battles between the Mods and Rockers in the '60s were inflamed, if not actually initiated, by the press. Football hooliganism too, especially when teams travel overseas, may have been exaggerated and in part provoked by the press.

But the violence, when it does occur, is real, and so far nobody has managed to prevent it. Should the reaction be tough or soft?

Young people who dress in an unorthodox way are frequently stopped by the police.

> 'He's got a heart of gold. Forget that funny hair.'
>
> Mother of a Punk

The drugs

The use of drugs such as opium and laudanum was tolerated in the nineteenth century. In the USA, the first serious anti-drug legislation was passed in 1914. Supporters of the new law claimed it would solve every kind of problem – 'from unemployment and crime in the street to preserving the white race'.

> 'That humanity... will ever be able to dispense with artificial paradises seems unlikely.'
> Aldous Huxley in The Doors of Perception

Today, despite anti-drug laws in almost every country, the use of drugs continues to grow. The list includes amphetamines, barbiturates, psychedelic drugs like LSD, glue-sniffing and massive use of cannabis (also known as pot, hash, marijuana, ganja etc.).

It is increasingly maintained that cannabis is not particularly harmful to the taker, but heroin and some other drugs can most certainly kill. Argument continues over the physical effects of glue-sniffing and LSD.

> 'A gun in your right hand, a joint in your left.'
> Student slogan, 1968

Drugs are blamed for antisocial lifestyles. The use of 'ganja' as a sacred drug by Rastafarians has helped alienate young blacks from the police. Hard-drug addicts are accused of violent, dangerous and criminal behaviour. And the criminal underworld, including the Mafia, are heavily involved in this lucrative trade.

The traditional remedy is to repress drug use with the force of law. Another approach is to legalize the less dangerous drugs and provide treatment for addicts.

Putting on the pressure? Narcotic squads are active throughout the world in the attempt to catch and deter drug users, clamp down on the 'pushers' or drug sellers and, internationally, to prevent drug smuggling and even the growth of plants from which some drugs are made. In the '70s, for example, the US government temporarily persuaded Turkey to outlaw poppy growing (for heroin and opium) in exchange for large cash payments.

Smuggling rings are sometimes broken, with much publicity based on the alleged 'street value' of the drugs captured. Pushers get heavy sentences, though convicted drug users are generally treated more leniently.

Critics of this approach claim that it does not work. Most drugs remain available. Where supplies are successfully restricted, the price rises. This may lead to dangerous adulteration of the drug. Price rises also draw yet more serious criminals into the supply system in the hope of high rewards.

Going easy? In 1978 the Dutch government declared cannabis 'relatively innocuous' and made its use legal. 'Our aim was to turn it into an unsensational item', said a government spokesman. It is claimed that less than two per cent of the population are now regular users.

An attempt to ease up over heroin in Amsterdam has proved to be more controversial. Meanwhile, Amsterdam's serious crime rate went up sharply and police blamed the heroin community.

Events in Holland have been interpreted as strengthening the call for the legalization of cannabis and suggesting that heroin should be controlled by law while treatment is offered.

The central argument against any relaxation on drugs is that their use is immoral and a vice, and should on no account be condoned by society.

Opposite A young drug addict injects himself in full view of passers-by.

dilemma

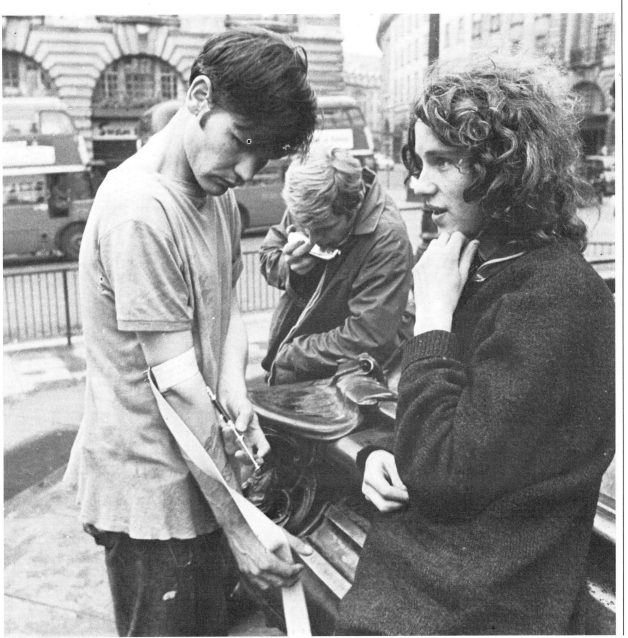

Abortion –

One of the most hotly fought debates in the field of personal morality and its interpretation in public law is the issue of abortion.

In the USA in 1973 the Supreme Court ruled that a woman, in consultation with her doctor, could have a legal abortion in the first 12 weeks of pregnancy. The state could not interfere with her decision regarding her own body. In Britain and in many other parts of the Commonwealth the law states that a woman may terminate her pregnancy if continuing it would involve a greater risk to her life than stopping it. Injury to her health can also justify abortion. Sometimes her economic welfare may also be taken into account. Very often however, under the law, a final decision rests with one or more doctors.

> **'An unborn baby is a human being.'**
> *Anti-abortionist*

Most countries now allow abortion in restricted circumstances. The tightest restrictions are in Muslim and Catholic societies. Worldwide it is estimated that 55 million abortions take place every year.

Massacre of the innocents? Those who oppose abortion believe that the foetus at conception is a living human being and that abortion is therefore murder. They also say that a society which holds life cheap is morally impoverished. The Catholic Church and other religious faiths in particular are deeply opposed to abortion.

Many anti-abortionists see abortion as just another method of contraception used by frivolous women in an age of sexual permissiveness. Tales are told of aborted foetuses crying as they are sluiced away and women suffering permanent physical and psychological damage as a result of the operation. At the same time, childless couples wait desperately to adopt a baby – since the legalization of abortion, the number of babies available for adoption has dropped sharply.

A respect for life? The abortion debate is inextricably linked with women's rights movements. Those who want to liberalize the law generally base their arguments on a woman's rights over her own body. Far from being anti-life, they claim, their slogan 'Every child a wanted child' shows how much they care about the quality of life in an overpopulated world.

PROTECT UNBORN CHILDREN

ABORTION KILLS

another name for murder ?

In reply to the charge that abortion is murder, the reformers ask, 'When does life begin? At conception?' If so, widely accepted methods of contraception like the pill or the intra-uterine devices which may involve the loss of a fertilized egg are technically instruments of murder.

But is it murder to abort a baby which is viable (likely to live though premature)? One of the difficulties in law is to determine the point of viability. In most countries it is set between 24 and 28 weeks, but with advanced medical technology it could be much earlier. The status of test tube babies also raises problems.

No easy answer? These are difficult issues for both sides. In response to the growing acceptance of abortion, the pro-life lobby has hardened its case and is fighting to outlaw abortion in almost all circumstances. The supporters of abortion are continuing their campaign to allow the pregnant woman the choice of whether to continue her pregnancy.

'If men got pregnant, abortion would be easy.' *Pro-abortionist*

PROTECT UNBORN CHILDREN

SOCIAL JUSTICE— NOT KILLING

PROTECT UNBORN CHILD

ABORTION KILLS BABIES

After the liberalization of the '60s, when abortion became more easily available in many countries, anti-abortion campaigners have tried to reverse the tide by public demonstrations.

Euthanasia – killing for kindness?

Euthanasia literally means a 'quiet and easy death'. Yet, in modern society, to help someone to achieve such a death is classed as murder.

In other cultures and other times, a choice of how one died was as valid as a choice of how one lived. The Roman philosopher Seneca said: 'If I can choose between a death of torture or one that is simple and easy, why should I not select the latter? As I choose the ship in which I sail and the house which I inhabit so I will choose the death by which I leave life.'

In 1961 it ceased to be illegal to commit suicide in Britain. But to help another person commit suicide remains a criminal offence throughout the world. Recent trends in Holland, however, suggest that voluntary euthanasia may soon be legalized there.

> **'Keeping him alive may not be best for him.'**
> *Consultant physician, Ottawa, Canada*

An easy death? Pressure groups everywhere are now seeking to change the law. They want to make it legal for people to authorize a doctor or attendant to allow them to die or to speed their death with medication when they feel their life has become intolerable. They suggest that a declaration to this effect should be drawn up, rather like a will, witnessed by two people. This paper can be revoked at any time just by tearing it up or issuing counter instructions. This proposal has not become law although in recent years many cases of 'mercy killing' have not been prosecuted.

Those who oppose euthanasia rest their argument on the idea that only God has the power of life and death. They argue that doctors and nurses, committed to preserving life, should not have to do anything so morally repugnant as administer a fatal dose to a patient.

If patients are so distraught on hearing that they have a certain disease that they beg for death and later it is discovered that the diagnosis was wrong, who will take responsibility for that death? And what about the risk of pressure from unscrupulous relatives who might benefit from their death and persuade them to sign a form?

The quality of life? The supporters of voluntary euthanasia point out that only a minority practise a religion. Why then should the majority be bound by laws based on religious concepts? The Catholic Church itself runs many hospices for dying people, and the Vatican has directed that pain-killing drugs can be administered to relieve suffering, even at the risk of shortening life. All those who treat terminally ill patients recognize that there is a very grey area between relieving pain and actively stopping it for good.

Doctors have always regarded the preservation of the patient's life as their absolute duty. But now, when the average adult in developed countries has so long a lifespan and when we can be kept technically alive on machines long after our brains have died, maybe mere survival should give way to a consideration of the *quality* of life. However, a great burden of responsibility would then fall on medical staff who would have to make the decision. Is that fair?

Opposite An old person in a hospital ward. Should she have the right to decide to die?

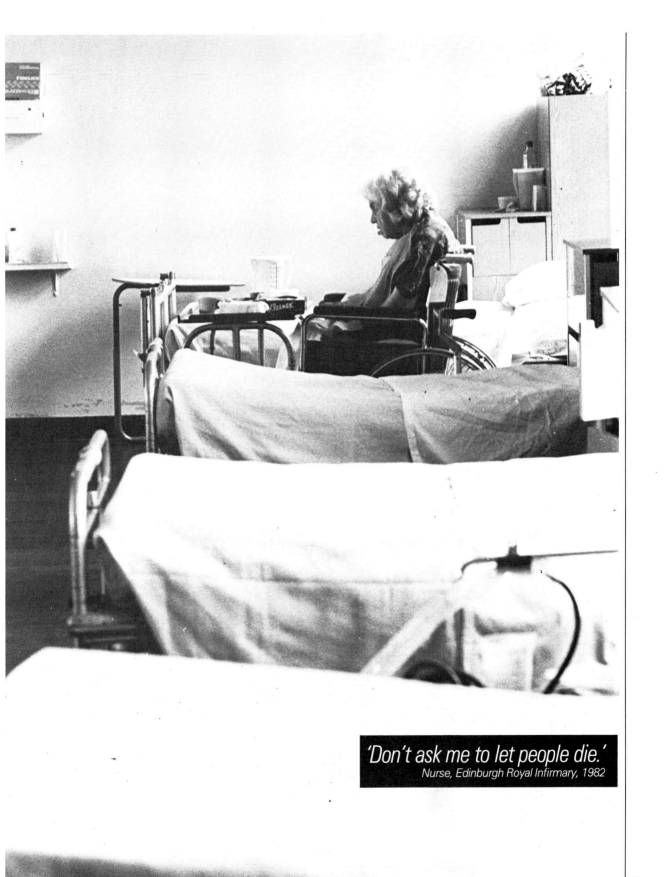

'Don't ask me to let people die.'
Nurse, Edinburgh Royal Infirmary, 1982

Forced

ost of us, from cradle to grave, accept quite a high level of state control in our lives. Laws govern the way we are educated, the standard of our housing, the conditions of our employment, the constituents of our food and the state of our environment.

Some people think that laws control too many aspects of our lives, leaving little room for personal initiative. Others see government control as vital for our safety and well-being.

Why should I use a seat-belt? In many countries it is now compulsory for a driver and the front-seat passenger in a car to use a seat-belt. In Australia back-seat passengers must also wear them. Yet before these laws were introduced, many objected strongly that this represented an intolerable infringement of their rights as free people.

The argument for compulsory use of seat-belts was based both on the hope of saving life and the high cost of death on the road. It is estimated that each fatal road accident costs the community some £150,000.

This was enough to persuade legislators in countries such as Australia and Canada where people take their personal freedom seriously. Britain followed in 1983. The result of these laws has been a dramatic drop in serious injuries in road accidents, in some cases up to 25 per cent.

A ban on cigarettes? It is now beyond doubt that smoking is a major cause of bronchitis, heart disease and lung cancer. The cost of caring for victims is very high – as much as £3 a year for every man, woman and child in the community. But there is still no law against smoking.

Many governments now insist that cigarette packets should carry a health warning, and smoking is increasingly banned in public places. But critics say governments are more interested in the taxes on tobacco than in saving life or cutting hospital costs. Smokers defend their right to smoke as a personal freedom.

What about alcohol? Many people have stopped smoking cigarettes. But consumption of alcohol is increasing.

Alcohol abuse leads to ill health, both

> ## 'It's a free country, isn't it?'
> *Young smoker*

to be safe?

physical and psychological, and to the disruption of family and working life. Thirty-three per cent of all divorce petitions in Britain cite alcohol as a contributory factor. It is estimated that eight million working days are lost every year through alcohol abuse.

The connection between alcohol and criminality is also well-established. A special report by the US Department of Health, Education and Welfare in 1978 states that alcohol was involved in some way in the crimes of 83 per cent of the prison population.

In the 1920s the USA temporarily and unsuccessfully prohibited alcohol. Many religious bodies have launched temperance movements against 'the demon drink'. But today its use is socially acceptable in most Western countries.

In a few countries like Norway, Sweden and Canada, it is quite difficult to buy alcohol, and the drink-driving laws are fierce. One argument says this is dreary puritanism, the other that it is sober good sense. The question is, which matters most – an individual's right to please himself, or the potential cost to the community?

Nine people died and twenty were injured in this motorway pile-up. In making safety regulations compulsory, is society striking the correct balance between law and liberty?

'He was drunk and he ran her down, the bastard.'
Witness of an accident

Free speech –

Freedom of speech and the freedom of thought that goes with it are defended as fundamental human liberties. Democracies consider free speech essential to the election of representative governments, and free discussion provides impetus for reform and social progress.

But it is generally agreed there must be some limits. The law of libel, for example, is meant to stop people maliciously damaging the reputation of others. But what about obscenity? What about censorship in the arts? Should one racial group be allowed to preach intolerance of another in the name of freedom? Even more important, perhaps, how far should people be allowed to go in attacking government and constitution?

Protest or subversion? The more liberal-minded a government, the greater the freedom it gives its citizens to attack the powers that be. This may extend to allowing hostile demonstrations and prohibiting only the betrayal of the state to foreign governments.

At the same time the security forces of these countries keep watch on people with extreme political views so that freedom, in effect, is practised on licence.

Some countries, however, make few efforts

> 'Congress shall make no law … abridging the freedom of speech or of the press.'
> First amendment to the US Constitution, 1791

Western countries pride themselves on freedom of speech. At Speakers' Corner in Hyde Park, London, people are traditionally allowed to express extreme views, though they are still subject to the ordinary law.

how free?

to maintain political liberty. In South Africa, for example, some protesters who claimed that the constitution discriminated against non-whites have faced trial for treason.

A free press? The right of newspapers and the other media to report and comment freely on all aspects of society and all activities of government is held to be a basic part of the democratic process. But newspapers are often charged with abusing their freedom by paying criminals for their revelations (cheque-book journalism) or by intruding on privacy. And they frequently run into trouble with angry governments.

The media are accused of concentrating on the negative side of life and ignoring positive developments. Many Third World countries, where press freedom is restricted, say the Western system allows sensationalism and distortion.

Another problem is press ownership, which is often in the hands of a small group of individuals. Does freedom of the press mean simply freedom for these few people to express their ideas?

In totalitarian countries, what appears in the papers often has to go through the hands of government censors first. But even in countries with no outright censorship, journalists may be afraid to write the truth as they see it and so practise a self-censorship that can be just as effective.

Press freedom, then, is often controversial and may sometimes be an illusion. Television, because of its immense power, is generally even more closely controlled, and in many countries is actually run by the state.

Censoring the arts? Almost all countries, in the name of religion or decency, put some restriction on the arts. But because this can mean suppression of serious and important work, an increasing number of people believe there should be no restrictions at all.

Those who accept restraint have to ask themselves whether interference by law or other public authority should come before or after publication or performance. Where it occurs before, as in many countries, this is open censorship. The alternative is to prosecute *afterwards* if the ordinary laws of obscenity, libel etc. have been broken. This is the practice in more liberal countries.

'Ban this degrading filth.'
Anti-pornography campaigner

Hitler addresses a mass rally shortly before the Second World War (1939-45). His denunciation of the Jews led directly to the Holocaust in which six million of them died. Does free speech mean that the incitement of racial hatred should be allowed?

27

Torture – can it

It has been estimated that in recent years over 60 countries have used torture against their citizens. They include South Africa, Chile, Indonesia, South Korea, Iraq and Iran.

But it is not only totalitarian or military governments that use torture. The French used it in Algeria, the Americans used it in Vietnam, and in 1973 the British were found guilty of the use of torture in Northern Ireland by the Court of Human Rights in Strasbourg.

Because it is outside the law, disowned by both national governments and international agencies, torture is conducted in secret. The state breaks the law, ostensibly for the purpose of upholding it.

A regrettable necessity? No one admits to using torture. It is called 'intensive interrogation'. The justification is always that information has to be extracted quickly from prisoners, against their will, to save innocent lives. It is a regrettable fact that bombings, hijackings and assassination attempts may only be prevented if vital information is gained in time.

People who want to outlaw the use of torture completely claim that it is also used in far less dramatic situations to create fear and discourage opposition. In Korea, for example, students demonstrating against the government were beaten, tortured and then released without charge. The government had made its point.

Below This man was most grievously tortured before death.

> '*Torture which is invoked to defend the state in effect destroys it.*'
> *Malise Ruthven in* Torture, the Grand Conspiracy, *1978*

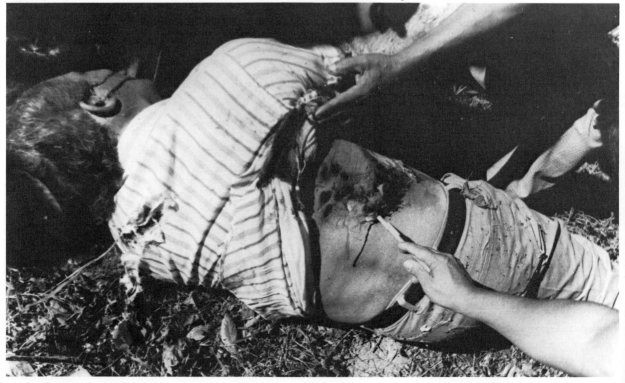

be justified?

Campaigners for human rights claim that torture is widely used to wipe out opposition to the government. The Ba'ath Party in Iraq is cited as an example of a régime maintained by secret police and the use of torture.

The victims of torture are not always political activists. They may include students, teachers, nuns, priests, women and children. In El Salvador, between January and August 1980, it is estimated that over 6,000 people were killed by security forces, many of them after torture. This pattern is common in Central America.

A well-documented infringement of human rights in South America is the 'disappearance' of thousands of people thought to be critics of the government. They are taken at night by anonymous men in civilian clothes and never seen again. In Argentina, in the first few years after the military junta took over in 1976, it is estimated that 24,000 people 'disappeared' in this way.

> ## 'We have to pay for security. It doesn't come cheap.'
> CIA official

Order without law? The international human rights organization, Amnesty International, believes that the routine use of torture is widespread. Ironically, it is mostly inflicted on people who have no information that could possibly be useful to the police or security forces.

The human rights campaigners argue that torture may initially be used for a short-term specific purpose but that it quickly becomes part of an unquestioned system of repression. In the words of one campaigner, 'It destroys the rule of law in the name of order.'

The organization points to increasingly sophisticated methods which make torture harder to detect. Drugs, electric shocks and sensory deprivation leave few physical scars but devastating psychological effects.

The fundamental argument against torture is that it is an assault on human dignity which no one can condone. Yet many states use it systematically to enforce law and order and feel justified in doing so.

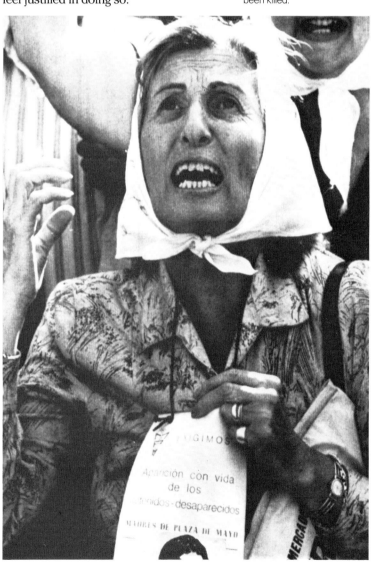

An Argentinian mother calls for the return of her vanished son. The sign around her neck reads: 'We demand that the arrested and disappeared persons appear alive.' But many thousands had already been killed.

Terrorist

It is a truism of the twentieth century that terrorists can overnight become respected leaders of governments.

Pandit Nehru of India, Jomo Kenyatta of Kenya and Robert Mugabe of Zimbabwe all spent time in gaol as terrorists while fighting for their countries' independence. As a young man, Menachem Begin masterminded terrorist activities against the British, including the bombing of the headquarters of the British army in Jerusalem in 1946. Nearly 100 people died. He became the Prime Minister of Israel.

Criminals? Or political idealists? Most of the acts of terrorism that we are familiar with involve bombings, hijackings and kidnappings committed by people who want political change. They use the fear their methods cause and the publicity they gain to bring pressure on the government they oppose. Terrorists of both the extreme right and the extreme left of the political spectrum are united in their belief that the end justifies the means.

In the 1970s the Baader Meinhof group created havoc in West Germany with their campaign of violence and bombings against the 'tyranny of the state'. They were helped by the Palestinian Liberation Organization (PLO), a terrorist group founded to assert the territorial rights of the Palestinian people against the state of Israel.

The Provisional Irish Republican Army is the terrorist faction of the movement for a united Ireland. Their policy of bombings and sectarian murders came to a head in November 1974 when they planted a bomb in a Birmingham pub, killing 20 people and injuring many more. For many they were nothing but a bunch of thugs and criminals terrorizing ordinary people. Their attempt to bomb the entire British government in Brighton in September 1984 was said to be just another indication of their desire to destroy democratic government.

The IRA, naturally, see things differently: they are a group of people with legitimate political aspirations who have not been able to achieve them by constitutional means because the constitution has been loaded against them. They point to the deprived state of the Catholic areas of Northern Ireland, and the continuing imbalance of civil rights between Catholic and Protestant. And they claim their effectiveness is due to the high

= patriot?

level of popular support they enjoy in the province.

A problem without frontiers? Terrorist groups throughout the world form a network of international terrorism. They often share training, resources and information. With the growing ease of communication, one country's battles are increasingly imported and fought out within another's borders; foreign nationals are assassinated, planes are hijacked. If the aim of the terrorists is to spread terror, then with media coverage the entire world becomes their stage.

Governments seek to cooperate with each other in resisting terrorist demands, but this is not always successful. Their efforts to prevent terrorist activities with increasing use of surveillance techniques may affect the civil liberties of ordinary citizens.

> *'Terrorists use violence. The state uses legitimate force.'*
> Conor Cruise O'Brien, newspaper editor

Funerals become a display of rebellion against the state. Members of the Irish National Liberation Army (INLA), one of the outlawed Republican groups in Northern Ireland, escort a dead comrade to the cemetery.

A right to

T hough many people break the law at times, they generally live law-abiding lives, whether through acceptance of the moral values of society or through fear of the consequences of breaking the law. But this does not mean that they necessarily find all laws just.

What they can do about any differences of opinion with the law depends very much on the kind of society they live in. In some totalitarian states, constant criticism of a government may put individuals outside the law and cause them to be labelled deviants or traitors and punished accordingly. Liberal democracies, on the other hand, pride themselves on being able to tolerate and absorb criticism. Opposition parties, pressure groups and peaceful protest can all be used to influence policy.

But what happens when the pressure and the protest achieve nothing? Is it ever right to break the law?

Civil disobedience Mahatma Gandhi launched a campaign of civil disobedience in 1919 to try and remove British colonial administration from India. He led a movement of passive resistance, urging people to defy and break laws which he felt were unjust, but without the use of force.

The Civil Rights movement led by Dr Martin Luther King in the '60s in the USA also used passive resistance. Black people broke the laws of states which practised racial segregation by using restaurants, buses and public facilities set apart for whites only. They began to attend schools and colleges from which they had been barred.

In 1964 the USA passed a Civil Rights Bill, its first, to outlaw racial discrimination in hous-

> ## 'Crime is created by the law.' *Social scientist*

The eminent philosopher Bertrand Russell led the earliest British demonstrations in favour of unilateral nuclear disarmament. He and his followers practised civil disobedience by staging mass sit-downs in public places.

break the law?

ing, education and employment. Those who had broken laws and been prosecuted for it felt they had contributed towards this success.

Today protesters against the use of nuclear weapons often fall foul of the law. There have been serious clashes between the police and demonstrators, especially in Japan and Germany. Women who were camping out on Greenham Common in England to protest against Cruise missiles often found themselves in court – either because they had openly defied the law by attempting to break into the base, or because they were camping on private land.

The right response? Many people disapprove deeply of such behaviour. They may or may not agree with the policies of the anti-nuclear campaigners, for example, but they refuse to accept that it is ever right to break the law. Individuals should not claim the right to decide which laws they will respect and which they will not. This is paving the way, they argue, for the breakdown of civilized society, with the rule of law giving way to anarchy.

They also claim that those who deliberately break the law on ideological grounds are naive. They are providing a vehicle for unscrupulous political agitators whose aim is to destroy society.

Finally there is the argument that those who break the laws of constitutionally elected governments may put their own aims in danger. For they have opened a path for others at a later date to bring about the downfall of policies of which they themselves approve by using these same unconstitutional methods.

'Live by the law or live in fear.'
US judge, nineteenth century

Civil Rights demonstrators in the USA, 1963. Their mass movement changed history by ensuring greater equality for the black population. But the struggle for complete equality continues.

33

Is law for ever?

Opposite The German concentration camp at Belsen. The starving figure in the foreground is surrounded by the dead. Yet these horrors took place under the rule of Nazi law.

Governments encourage their citizens to believe in the sanctity of law. But it is remarkable how quickly the law changes. A study in the USA in 1931 showed that 76 per cent of prisoners had been convicted of offences which had not been illegal 16 years before.

In Britain the number of possible offences has increased from 2,000 to 7,000 in the past 45 years. Some crimes have disappeared as others have arrived. Swearing was technically a criminal offence in England and Wales up to 1966. Suicide was a crime from 1854 to 1961. Incest has only been a crime since 1908.

> '*We hold these truths to be self-evident, that all men are created equal.*'
> *American Declaration of Independence, 1776*

How then can a citizen feel respect for laws that change like the weather, sometimes with doubtful justice and sometimes also to the benefit of one section of the community at the expense of another?

Making the laws we need? Finance provides one example of the way law can be used for administration. Parliament, Congress or Assembly will decide upon an annual budget. The agreed measures are converted into a set of financial laws that may last only a year. The law is functioning as part of the machinery of government.

Another common use for law is to achieve social reform. Education provides numerous examples. In Spain it is now the legal right of

> '*Without justice, what is a state but a robber band?*'
> *St Augustine in* The City of God

all who are qualified to attend university. The aim is to extend the benefits of education as widely as possible through all social classes.

In the USA, Congress and presidents have used the law to set up special programmes aimed at reducing educational disadvantage among young children. Attempts are being made in a number of countries to establish equality for all races by legislation. The law is being used to achieve specific objectives.

Law greater than government? Long before the use of law for administration and reform, there was a general belief that laws to govern human conduct came from God or depended on the very nature of the universe. Like God and nature, they were fixed and eternal.

Religious law, as in Christian or Muslim systems, tended to be very conservative. The idea of 'natural' law developed until philosophers began to claim that people had basic rights and should not be deprived of them. This was literally a revolutionary way of thinking. It formed the basis of the American Declaration of Independence of 1776 and the French Revolution of 1789.

The grotesque misuse of law by some twentieth-century dictatorships has led to a comeback for the idea of natural law. This may be seen in the United Nations Declaration of Human Rights. The alleged over-permissiveness and moral failure of the modern world has also led some Muslim states to return to a very early, fundamentalist version of Islamic religious law. In one or two countries this includes the practice of cutting off the hands of thieves. Religious and natural law can be either a modernizing or a reactionary force.

Many people who defy their governments believe they are acting in the name of a higher morality and a greater law, either natural or religious.

What laws do

Adults break the law with extraordinary frequency. A whole series of surveys and research reports has shown that between 75 and 92 per cent of them habitually add to their incomes in ways that are illegal, technically at least. In a survey of 1,700 Americans, 91 per cent said they had committed at least one offence they could have gone to prison for. It seems probable that just as many young people commit offences, serious and petty.

And yet most people, whatever their age and however they behave, consider themselves decent, reasonable, law-abiding citizens. What laws, then, do *you* break? Why? And do you think that you are justified?

Are we all thieves? Many people have a strong objection to stealing. Yet in a study of 1,400 schoolboys, over 90 per cent admitted to having stolen something. Sweets and cigarettes were particular targets.

In certain countries, particularly Britain, convictions for shoplifting are on the up and up. In some other European countries, however, it is no longer a criminal offence. This leniency stems from a growing feeling that modern forms of self-service selling actively encourage dishonesty by their tempting displays of easily accessible goods.

Other very common forms of stealing include employees helping themselves to small items at work. The theft of stationery is rife, as is the making of private calls on office telephones. And the removal of toilet paper is so commonplace that in the lavatories of government offices the words 'Government Property' are often stamped on every single sheet in an attempt to embarrass thieves.

Getting away with it? Young people's misdemeanours may range from naughtiness to real crime, by way of pastimes like under-age drinking which are completely acceptable within youth culture, whatever the attitude of authority.

At the most trivial end are games like ringing doorbells and running away before anyone can answer. Breaking glass, removing petrol caps, snapping off car aerials and damaging plants are all very common. This kind of behaviour can escalate into costly vandalism which makes parts of many cities even more disagreeable than they were to

> '**The council closed the only official play space because of vandalism.**'
> *Community social worker, 1974*

you break?

begin with. Young people also commit many motoring offences like driving without licence or insurance, and joy-riding in stolen cars.

The same motoring offences are by no means unknown among adults. But adults are probably more prone than young people to driving after one drink too many, exceeding the speed limit and systematically breaking parking regulations in the hope of getting away with it.

Where do you stand? If you have a tendency to these or any other misdemeanours, it is worth considering your own attitude to the law and order debate. Have you behaved badly or done anything illegal? Do you feel guilty? How much is done to impress mates? How much arises from boredom or a deprived environment? Will you be doing it again? Would you do it if you knew you would be caught? What will you feel if you are caught? And will the law be right if it punishes you?

> *'We go nicking every dinner hour. All of us do it.'*
> *Schoolboy, 1980*

Few people feel guilty about parking offences. Yet parking in the wrong place can create considerable problems in modern cities.

The police –

One of the main problems facing a democratic society is how to use its police force to protect citizens from crime and disorder without taking away their right to behave as they wish. Some argue that without the police there would be no freedom at all. Others say the police are more concerned with control than they are with liberty.

But the police have an enormous range of other duties outside crime and public order. These, too, affect the way that people see them.

Your friendly policeman? Inevitably, people's reaction to the police has much to do with their own personal experience. Research shows that those living in well-kept suburbs or richer neighbourhoods trust and like the police more than those living in poorer areas, especially the inner cities.

The British *Police Instruction Book*, issued in the nineteenth century, stated that 'the primary object of an efficient police force is the *prevention* of crime; the next that of detection and punishment of offenders if crime is committed.' Recruits still memorize these words.

In fact, the police forces in most countries now also control crowds and traffic, protect politicians, diplomats and important foreign visitors, deal with lost property, break the news of death to families and help in every kind of emergency. One-third of all calls to the police in the USA are for help where no crime is involved.

Most members of the police come from families who are not well-off, but sociologists have shown that they acquire middle-class attitudes to property and obedience during their working lives. There is no evidence that those who join the police have specially authoritarian personalities at the point of

In many communities police are invited into schools to dispel prejudice and help children to understand their role. Sometimes, as in this picture, the result can be a happy one outside school as well.

friend or foe?

joining. But some recruits at least may be attracted by fast cars and the hope of an exciting working life.

A justified fear? To many people the sight of a police uniform causes fear and an uneasy feeling of guilt, whether deserved or not. In practice, most meetings between police and public are to do with motoring, and this has undoubtedly had a bad effect on the public's view of the police.

Another pressure point is the relationship between police and young people. Police are accused of being automatically suspicious of young people, particularly if they belong to ethnic minorities. They are also accused of indiscriminate searches of youngsters, using this as a way of disciplining and controlling young people rather than directly trying to deal with crime.

Even more serious is the charge that the

> *'The police have to be seen and see themselves as protectors of liberty within the law.'*
> John Alderson, former Chief Constable

police may themselves be prepared to bend the law in order to keep down crime and anti-social behaviour. Studies in the US have shown that police see themselves as law and order 'craftsmen', entitled to do what they think fit to maintain public order, and often unwilling to accept the restrictions placed on them by the courts.

Police in many countries have been found guilty of planting evidence and extracting confessions under duress. This may indicate an enthusiasm to control people whom they consider wrongdoers. But when it happens, it greatly undermines public confidence in the police.

The camera catches the rough edge of police behaviour during the disturbances in Brixton, London, in 1981.

Can the police

Revolutionaries welcome crime as a sign of the disintegration of society. But, for everybody else, the question is how to control it. Should the battle be fought hard and furious, possibly at the cost of alienating the public? Or should the approach be 'softly, softly'? And should citizens take a hand in helping the police?

Forward to the revolution? For those who believe that crime is a clearsighted response to society's injustices, the only way to prevent it is through radical reform or revolution.

Yet crime still remains a problem in many countries that have passed through revolutionary change. Official corruption has been the target of massive campaigns in the USSR in recent years. Even China, generally viewed as an orderly nation since the end of the Cultural Revolution, acknowledged in 1978 that it had serious crime problems. Since then some criminals have been shot in public as an example.

Many people have come to believe there will always be an element of crime in modern society, however it is organized, so a vigilant police force will always be needed.

Waging war on crime? Calls for tough action in the war on crime have been particularly strong in recent years, and police forces have generally grown in numbers.

Changes in policing style have also taken place. From the mid-'60s police patrols began to give way to 'unit policing' – fast response in cars, directed by police radio. This change from prevention before the event to reaction afterwards is called 'fire-brigade policing'.

> 'The only way to cut out crime is by unacceptable repression.'
> *Criminologist*

cope?

A new police tactic now used worldwide is to meet civil disturbance with massed forces of police. Here, pickets arrive at the Orgreave coking plant during the British miners' strike of 1984-85 to find their way barred by a massive police presence.

'Law and order is a joint exercise between the people and the police.' Sir David McNee, Metropolitan Police

Police forces also set up special units to deal with particular types of crime like drugs or fraud, and also to tackle particular areas where crime was serious. One tactic came to be called 'saturation policing'. It involved placing great numbers of officers on the street at once. And it was one such operation, described later in Lord Scarman's official report as a 'serious mistake', which triggered major disturbances in Brixton, London, in 1981. There have also been battles, with many deaths, between police and demonstrators in countries as different as Japan and the USA.

Critics call confrontation with the civilian population 'military policing', and believe we will see more of it in all parts of the world. It involves the deployment of the police in large numbers, and their increasing use of an aggressive, hit-first policy.

Turning to the community Inevitably any tendency to 'military policing' arouses hostility in the community and may cut off the flow of information from the public which is so vital for the prevention of crime and detection of criminals. So new ways of strengthening links between police and community are being sought.

A remarkable 'Neighbourhood Watch' scheme in Detroit in the USA involved the setting-up of a network of 'civilians' who reported anything suspicious direct to the police. The result of this, and more police accessibility in general, was a 58 per cent drop in crime between 1977 and '79.

The model has been followed in many other experiments. Both the police and members of the public are alarmed, however, at the idea of vigilantes working independently of the police. This stirs unhappy memories of lynch mobs hanging or otherwise harming their victims.

In Britain, police-community liaison work is now obligatory, and many see this as one hopeful development.

Should the police

I t is the common assumption of almost every nation that the police should carry arms. Norway, Sweden and Britain still hold out against this view. What happens when the police do carry guns? And will it soon happen everywhere?

Winning by vulnerability? The most important argument in favour of unarmed police concerns public support. People with guns, whether police or civilians, are a lot less lovable than those without. According to Ben Whittaker, author of a book about policing, 'most British police officers are convinced that as soon as they were armed they would overnight lose much of the public's cooperation'. Unarmed police may in fact succeed by appearing weak.

> 'There is not the remotest likelihood of the police arming themselves for routine duties.'
> *Sir Robert Mark, Metropolitan Police, 1977*

Some people believe that if the police are armed, then criminals in turn will carry arms. Others say that an armed police force attracts a very different, and more aggressive kind of recruit.

Paying the price? In the USA the use of firearms is far more extensive than in any other developed nation. In proportion to the population there are four times as many homicide victims in the US as there are in Canada, five times as many as in Australia and 10 times as many as in Britain.

Police officers in the US, who carry arms at all times, are murdered at an even higher rate. An American police officer is 20 times more likely than a British one to come to a violent end. An average of 90 American policemen and women are murdered annually.

Right The use of firearms by criminals has increased dramatically. This bank robber, filmed unawares, is using a sawn-off shotgun.

> 'We have now, at its worst, a blue army on the streets with a licence to kill.'
> *Sarah Manwaring-White, television journalist, 1983*

be armed?

American police are always armed. This patrolman is making a ground-to-air call to the police helicopter just visible above the telephone wires.

Over 500 citizens are killed each year by the US police in 'justifiable' circumstances. Yet in Western societies the fatal use of guns by the police is accepted only as a last resort in order to save life. If the police shoot and kill without sufficient reason they will be guilty of murder or at least of manslaughter.

Holding out against guns? As the last sizable country in the world without an armed police force, the case of Britain is particularly important. Under mounting pressure, how much longer can she hold out?

Armed robberies rose from 34 in 1950 to 935 in 1977. By 1981 guns were carried by criminals or used to attack others on 2,164 occasions in London alone. Attacks by international terrorists and bombings by the IRA have also grown more numerous. In fact, police protecting diplomats and those on certain other duties already carry guns. Police officers may also be issued with firearms on special occasions.

Some say this has gone too far, and a number of incidents seem to confirm this view. The most famous was the attack on Stephen Waldorf, shot in mistake for a wanted man while driving his car down a London street in 1981. Waldorf lived, and the police who shot him were acquitted of the charges brought against them.

An attempt has since been made to tighten up on firearms but in 1982 it was revealed that police in Manchester had carried guns on regular patrol. Is Britain in practice already a long way down the road to an armed police force? If so a major principle is gradually being eroded without an official change in policy. Does this matter? What are the implications?

'In New York, officers in plain clothes have shot each other, each believing their colleague to be a criminal.'
Ben Whittaker in The Police in Society, 1982

Policing

One of society's nightmares is of a corrupt police force running out of control, making its own rules and enforcing them arbitrarily. Finding the best way of ensuring fair and effective policing, respecting the rights and wishes of the people, has long been a puzzle for Western nations.

Some people believe the police should be under the direct control of the government, others that control should be a local matter. There are also arguments over how to deal with corruption among the police themselves.

National policing? France has a national police force, two of them in fact. Australia and Canada have mixed systems of national and local forces. So does the USA, with many thousands of police forces representing different areas and levels of government, and a single, nationwide detective force, the Federal Bureau of Investigation (FBI). The head of the FBI is in theory a respected individual who stands outside party politics. In Britain the police are locally organized but subject to an important element of central control through the Home Office.

> 'It seemed to me of the first importance to get the weapon of the police into my own hands.'
> Herman Goering, Nazi Minister of Police, 1935

The main reason for not having a single police force is the fear that it could lead to totalitarian control, even to a coup. Supporters of national policing point out this has not happened in countries such as New Zealand and Denmark, both of which have national police. In 1962 the British Royal Commission on the police argued that what mattered was not the form of organization but the nature and intentions of the government.

The chief arguments in favour of national police are a gain in efficiency through centralized information and the chance to have a fair and even policing policy across the whole of a nation regardless of local interests.

Power to the people? Many believe that the way to bring humanity to the increasingly anonymous modern state is to return as many powers as possible to local communities. They argue that one of the main causes of disorder, and possibly crime as well, is that in run-down areas people feel they have no opportunity to determine their own lives.

the police?

If large numbers are outside politics, the argument goes, then they should be brought back in by better local democracy. This would include powers to give direction to the police.

Such thinking shocks those who believe the police force should be allowed to get on with the job with the minimum of interference – interference which could, they believe, involve meddling for political purposes by local politicians.

Protecting their own? It is beyond dispute that police officers and sometimes whole police forces can be corrupt. There have been spectacular instances of bribe-taking, planting of evidence, lying in court and violent behaviour by the police. No country can expect to be immune.

But who should police the police? The police forces themselves and their traditional allies have generally been content to let the police head their own inquiries, with the courts as a last resort. The counter-argument is that independent people should play a major part in investigating and disciplining the police.

A police force that rules the streets. Haiti's feared Ton Ton Macoutes stride through the capital, Port-au-Prince.

'When the law breaks the law, there is no law.'
Ramsey Clark, US Attorney General

A police

Many people fear the growth of police power in the Western state. The visible evidence of it comes from television where the riot police of many democratic countries are to be seen using apparently greater and greater force when public order is threatened. Nowadays the police use not just truncheons and horses but full riot gear, often backed by tear gas, water cannon and plastic bullets.

Many believe police aggression provokes still greater violence. There have been numerous deaths by police shooting in riots and demonstrations, most notably in Mexico, South Africa and the USA.

Under surveillance? Some critics, however, are even more alarmed by the invisible activities of the police. Most countries have

West Germany, 1983. White-helmeted police first make a pincer move to hem in anti-nuclear protesters; then the water cannon open up.

state?

specialized 'political' police whose job is to protect the government from subversion and espionage.

These special police are persistently accused of keeping records on people who take extreme political views of left or right, regardless of the fact that they may be acting entirely within their democratic rights. For example, records are often kept of people who attend legitimate political demonstrations, such as those against nuclear arms. Photographs and films are frequently taken and car numbers are noted.

Many police records are now kept on computer. These allow the amassing and instant interchange of many millions of items of information about millions of people. It is alleged that the information recorded is sometimes based on rumour and suspicion. In many countries Freedom of Information Acts give members of the public some access to their computerized files, but elsewhere they have no chance to refute possibly inaccurate information.

The police are also believed to be making increased use of telephone tapping (with spectacular effects in catching criminals in Australia); of film and video surveillance (which can record demonstrators as well as bank robbers); and even of camera surveillance by helicopter.

Justified by the need? Defenders of the police, and they are many, do not generally dispute the facts advanced by the critics.

They argue that these developments are a reasoned and reasonable response to increasingly difficult policing conditions. Disorder on the streets and at the factory gates has risen enormously and has to be contained. Likewise, they say, the danger from political subversion. Computers and other forms of modern technology are desperately needed to fight a mounting tide of crime and increasing peril to the state.

The critics are said to have nothing more to complain of than the occasional abuse or mistake. The police remain the servants of the democratic state.

'Contemporary crime demands up-to-date policing.'
Senior policeman

The courts are the key to any system of justice. It is their job to give a fair trial to those who come before them. But can they really do it? And how fair are the sentences they give?

Are judges impartial? Western countries, with their long tradition of justice, place great faith in the integrity of judges. But attention has concentrated recently on how they are appointed and the kind of people they are.

In the USA, many judges in the lower courts are elected just like politicians. To be re-elected they need to remain popular – this could threaten their impartiality. In Britain judges are appointed by, or at least on the advice of, the Lord Chancellor, the government's chief law officer. But even though they have been chosen by a politician, they are expected to remain absolutely independent and to serve the law as fairly as they can. All democratic countries expect this of their judges. It is extraordinarily difficult, however, to find a way of appointing them which does not leave them with a sense of gratitude or obligation to somebody.

Another problem is that judges, almost inevitably, are drawn from the professional classes. Might this not mean that they will have a narrow and conservative view of life because of their restricted backgrounds?

Right The dignity of the judiciary is emphasized by pomp and ceremony. These judges wear traditional robes and wigs. But how much do they have in common with those whose trials they will be conducting?

> **'I'll give you a fair trial and then hang you.'**
> *Sheriff in a Wild West movie*

Innocent or guilty? In theory a defendant is innocent until proved guilty. Most people who are accused of crimes in fact plead guilty before the trial begins. In such cases, the court's only job is sentencing.

Guilty pleas avoid unnecessary trials. But critics say they may arise when police have obtained a confession under pressure, or a defendant has been induced to plead guilty in the hope of a lighter sentence. Such 'plea bargaining' is bitterly criticised.

In recent years criminals have been encouraged to give evidence which has led to the conviction of other people, in the hope of reducing their own sentence. In Britain, they are known as 'supergrasses'. This system, too, is a source of criticism.

The courts prefer to let some guilty people go free rather than convict the innocent, thus upholding an important principle of justice. But the police believe too many guilty people

the courts fair?

are acquitted. Sir Robert Mark, a former senior policeman, wrote: 'There is no point in catching criminals if the system of trial is so inefficient that it lets them go free.'

Are sentences fair? The biggest arguments of all surround sentencing. Law and order campaigners say it is getting softer. They point to numerous examples, such as rape cases where the convicted man is only fined and not imprisoned. Yet some judges claim that prison sentences were shorter 30 years ago. Today the courts sometimes give unexpectedly harsh 'exemplary' sentences as a warning to others. In 1973 one boy of 16 got 20 years for his part in an act of robbery with violence.

> 'Soft judges aid and abet the criminal hooligan.'
> *Law and order campaigner, as quoted in the Sun, 1983*

The jury –

In trial by jury, a system 800 years old, a group of ordinary citizens are called upon to decide whether or not the person accused is guilty. The aim is for the community to retain some power over the law so that it cannot be used unjustly. But some argue that juries are bound to be inferior to expert judges, and want to see the system abolished. Among those who support the jury system, there are disagreements over central questions.

Representative of the people? In the past juries were often chosen only from the well-to-do. In Britain, for example, until 1973 jurors had to be over 21 and under 60 and either be house-owners or ratepayers. This meant they were worthy, middle-class and predominantly male, and might have little sympathy with large numbers of the accused.

Members of juries are now generally chosen at random by computer. But research has shown that women and immigrants of all nationalities are still under-represented. Those who want a fully democratic system are unhappy about this.

Yet it may be argued that young jurors lack a proper understanding of crime; that modern juries are sometimes ignorant because there is no educational qualification, and that they may include both the irresponsible and the inadequate.

Challenging the jury For a jury to be fair, its members should clearly be not only representative of the people but as free of prejudice as possible. In some countries, and particularly the USA, the defence is allowed to question

> 'It is good for a nation when its people feel that in the gravest matters justice belongs in part to them.'
> Lord Devlin, former High Court Judge, 1979

Waiting for a train. Any one of these people could be called upon to help determine the guilt or innocence of a fellow citizen.

citizens’ friend?

potential jurors freely about their beliefs. Many are rejected. In one case in 1971, 1,035 jurors were rejected before the hearing began.

Law and order campaigners often consider challenges an attempt to get rid of anyone who looks ‘respectable’, particularly in cases where the defendant is black, working-class or politically committed to the far left.

Those in favour of fully representative juries are equally angry when the prosecution obtains information against jurors from the police and security agencies. This can happen in cases involving political hostility to the established order. It is known as ‘jury vetting’.

Do juries get it right? Juries deliberate in secret and are not allowed to disclose what happened, even afterwards. Interesting comparisons have been made, however, between jury verdicts and the opinions of the judge and other court officials in particular cases. Usually all agree. But enough disagreement occurs to cause concern – even a small percentage of disagreement may mean that innocent people are being convicted.

In some countries, judges are allowed to accept a majority verdict. The main reason is police fear that individual jurors may be threatened or ‘nobbled’ by criminals. But majority verdicts also make it easier for juries to convict.

Jury vetting, majority verdicts, and transfer of some cases to non-jury courts are seen by critics as part of a campaign against the power of juries. E.P. Thompson, the historian, has accused those responsible of being ‘the muggers of the constitution and the vandals of the jury box’.

> ‘We preserve trial by jury because it’s a sacred cow.’
> *Professor Ben Hogan, criminal law expert, 1982*

Prison –

Prisons have existed for almost as long as society. Kings and rulers used them to confine their enemies. Later, they were also used to lock up wrongdoers such as thieves. The aims were to protect society, to assert the rule of law, to punish offenders and to deter others by example.

Repentance became one of the aims in the eighteenth century (prison was to be a place where wrongdoers would see the evil of their ways and regret them) – and so the American 'penitentiary' was born. Next, in the nineteenth century, came the idea of positive training to rehabilitate prisoners.

Modern society still uses prisons for all these reasons. But where do their priorities lie? And do they achieve their aims?

Do prisons cure criminals? Many people can only accept the idea of prison if it seems to be doing good. Attempts have been made, though rather patchily, to provide positive remedial training, mainly through welfare work and education. Some prisoners have even taken university degrees.

The facts suggest, however, that cases of rehabilitation are rare, that prison really is a university of crime, perhaps even an active cause of crime. Britain and the USA are among the four countries with proportionally the largest prison populations (the others are South Africa and Russia). In the USA, four-fifths of cleared-up crimes are committed by ex-prisoners. In Britain, over two-thirds of young offenders who have been held in custody are convicted again within two years.

Some argue that short sentences of three months or under may be beneficial, though the statistical evidence is rather shaky. There is better evidence that a court appearance alone can bring some offenders up sharp and scare them enough to prevent further offences.

A major enquiry for the Canadian parliament in 1977 stated emphatically that prison was 'a proven failure' in correcting criminals. This is an issue on which all sides increasingly agree.

Prison – a deterrent? The call for longer prison sentences is based in part on the hope that fear of prison will deter people from committing crime. Most of the facts indicate the opposite. Historically, harsher sentences for an offence have led to a slight drop followed by an increase in the crime. This was the sequence of events even with the restoration of capital punishment in some American states. Response to the current drink-drive laws is another example.

The evidence suggests that fear of getting caught is a greater deterrent than fear of prison.

Retribution? If rehabilitation and deterrence fail, then the strongest remaining arguments for prison are the protection of society and, simply, punishment.

With crime rates rising, prison clearly does little to protect society, except in the case of a few individuals such as compulsive killers or child molesters. But the idea of punishment has recently returned to fashion and has been the subject of a number of approving philosophical works. Some say the incarceration of human beings for punishment is unfitting for modern society. But there is a very widespread belief that those who have done wrong should be made to suffer.

> '*You might as well say cologne cures gangrene as to say prisons rehabilitate people.*'
> *Gary Smith, ex-prisoner, USA*

a university of crime?

'If vicious jailbirds suffer a little discomfort, are we supposed to weep?' Sun *newspaper, 1984*

Prisons in crisis?

In many countries prisons are said to be in crisis. Is this true? If so, is it a crisis that matters to society? And if it matters, what should be done? These questions provoke deep divisions.

Prison life Wherever one stands in the law and order debate there is no disagreement about the experience of prison – it's grim. In 1971 Jessica Mitford shocked America with her book *The American Prison Business*. This revealed, among other practices, the experimental use of drugs, brain surgery and psychiatric techniques to control 'violent'

Improving the situation? Some law and order advocates believe that prison should be as nasty as possible. Editorials in popular newspapers have urged judges to ignore overcrowding because bad conditions help to punish the offender. Prison services generally respond to bad conditions by seeking to build more and better prisons. But where this has happened, the prison population has quickly expanded to fill them.

Calls for more local prisons are often heard, in order to ease visiting problems. There are also pleas for more education in prisons.

> '*One sign of success in the fight for law and order is that more people are in prison.*' Merlyn Rees, former British Home Secretary

prisoners. In the USSR, where political dissidents are sometimes held in psychiatric hospitals, drugs are also freely used.

Worldwide, the gravest problems arise because, whatever the aims of imprisonment, once an offender is 'inside' the need for security and good order in the prison comes first. This may mean solitary confinement for the disruptive, up to 23 hours a day in cells for others, and endless roll calls and other forms of institutional control. Electronic surveillance of prisoners is also increasing.

Overcrowding is another great problem. Many prisoners live two, three or even more in cells built for one a century ago. Women seem to suffer particularly in prison – there have been instances of severe self-mutilation in what may sometimes seem the only available form of protest.

Prisons have other side effects. Some prisoners get so used to life inside that they become 'institutionalized' and cannot return to normal society. For many, imprisonment means marital breakdown and, in some cases, eventual homelessness.

Though law and order campaigners do not approve, a common government response to the prison crisis is to try to reduce the number of prisoners. Shorter prison sentences help but are difficult to implement when the judges and magistrates are not under direct government control.

Another way is to make use of alternative sentences such as suspended sentences, fines, probation orders and community service. Criminals may even be asked to make restitution to their victims by financial payments or by offering some personal service where this is acceptable.

A more controversial step is to 'decriminalize' certain offences. Some people say homeless alcoholics should be treated in centres, not sent to prison. Many advocate the 'decriminalization' of the possession and use of cannabis. In a number of European countries shoplifting is no longer a criminal offence.

But even so, the number of recorded crimes continues to rise. Few nations have been successful in achieving a real, long-term reduction in the number of prisoners.

Opposite Twentieth-century prisoners in a nineteenth-century prison. Overcrowding and shortage of staff make prison sentences even tougher than they might be.

A short,

The argument about the origins of crime and the best reaction to it is particularly intense in the case of young offenders. Many say their criminal behaviour springs from deliberate wickedness for which they should be punished, and cries in support of birching can still be heard.

Others are more inclined to attribute youthful crime to the pressures of society and particularly poverty of background – for which nobody can be blamed. Such people believe it is better to concentrate on treatment for young offenders rather than punishment, just as would be done with the mentally ill. They also argue that a child too young to know right from wrong cannot be accused of wickedness, and they would like to see the age of criminal responsibility raised rather than lowered.

Getting tough? Though many believe that the treatment of young delinquents has got softer, some countries are in fact using increasingly punitive methods. During the 1960s there seemed to be growing agreement that young people's offences should be treated as far as possible as non-criminal. Attempts were made to reduce the number of children under lock and key in favour of deferred sentences, supervision orders and attendance centres.

In recent years, however, the number passing through community homes and other places of detention has increased dramatically – in Britain, for example, there were five times as many in detention in 1981 as there had been in 1965. (The rise in juvenile crime can account for only one-fifth of this expansion.)

Brisker régimes are imposed on young-

The strict military-style régime in detention centres for young offenders is designed to promote discipline and respect for authority.

'Borstal taught me everything I know.'
Young offender

sharp shock?

sters in detention, with a greater emphasis on inspections and parades and less time devoted to training. Even so, the reconviction rate for those who have been held in secure institutions remains high – in some cases, as high as 80 per cent within two years.

Softly, softly? Some attempts are still being made to limit the incarceration of the young. In China, though adult thieves are sometimes shot, young offenders are often dealt with by counselling and mediation without police involvement. Police may decline to prosecute if they are hopeful about a young person's attitude.

In the USA, despite a strict approach in some states, overcrowding of penal institutions has encouraged 'community' responses in others. In Massachusetts virtually all the state's institutions for juveniles were closed down in the early '70s. The rate of offences, however, remained about the same. In other words the Massachusetts 'borstals' had not been holding down the juvenile crime rate – whatever they did for the inmates, they were doing little to protect the community.

Most people favouring a non-punitive approach would prefer young offenders to remain free but under supervision, so that they continue to live with their families while also under closer control. But this approach could mean increased surveillance of ordinary life by the agencies of the state. Those who object to this interference in the name of the greater liberty of society sometimes reach a paradoxical conclusion – that simple, old-fashioned punishment may in fact be better for the young offender.

A young man helps a disabled shopper. He is doing it voluntarily. Should young people who have broken the law be required to make amends through such community work?

The right

In recent years the trend has been for most European governments to abolish the death penalty for murder. By 1978, Austria, Finland, the Federal Republic of Germany, Iceland, Portugal and Sweden had abolished it completely. In Britain, although the death penalty remains on the statute book for treason, no one has been executed since 1964. A similar situation exists in many parts of the Commonwealth.

> *'An eye for an eye, and a tooth for a tooth.'*
> *St Matthew's Gospel*

The United Nations urges all countries to work towards abolishing capital punishment. However, even in countries where this has happened, large numbers of people are calling for its restoration.

Should murderers live? Supporters of the death penalty generally base their arguments on the principle of retribution: whoever takes another person's life should forfeit his own. This principle together with the passionate belief that only death is a just punishment for certain brutal crimes moves many people to support capital punishment. The judge Lord Denning called it 'the most emphatic denunciation by the community of a crime'.

Statistics do not prove that the death penalty deters murderers. On the other hand, supporters of the death penalty argue, they don't disprove it either. And it is better to be safe. Life imprisonment for convicted murderers is an unnecessary expense for the taxpayer, and for the offender may mean only a few comfortable years in prison with remission of sentence for good behaviour and early release on parole.

The only sure way to make society safe from murderers, they argue, is to remove them – permanently. And the only way to show that society values life is to demand the ultimate punishment for those who take life.

Murder by the state? Opponents of the death penalty condemn it as cruel, inhuman and degrading. It does not deter criminals, they say, but it brutalizes society. They predict the death penalty will go the way of disembowelling: once regarded as a just punishment but now, rightly, seen as barbaric.

Contrary to popular myth, they argue, most murder victims are killed by people they know, often members of their own family, in incidents which would never recur. The cold-blooded terrorist, on the other hand, would probably welcome execution in order to become a martyr and win publicity for his cause.

In 1983, 1,699 executions were officially recorded in 39 countries. The true figures are probably much higher. Some of these people had been subjected to torture before execution and the majority of procedures that led to execution 'fell short of international norms for a fair trial', in the opinion of human rights campaigners.

There is strong evidence to suggest that, in countries which have the death penalty, governments use it as a means of political control: the ultimate method of maintaining 'law and order'.

In sixteenth-century France, a criminal is about to be dismembered by the executioner. Scenes like this were a favourite public spectacle, and taken completely for granted – though today we would consider them barbaric.

to take life?

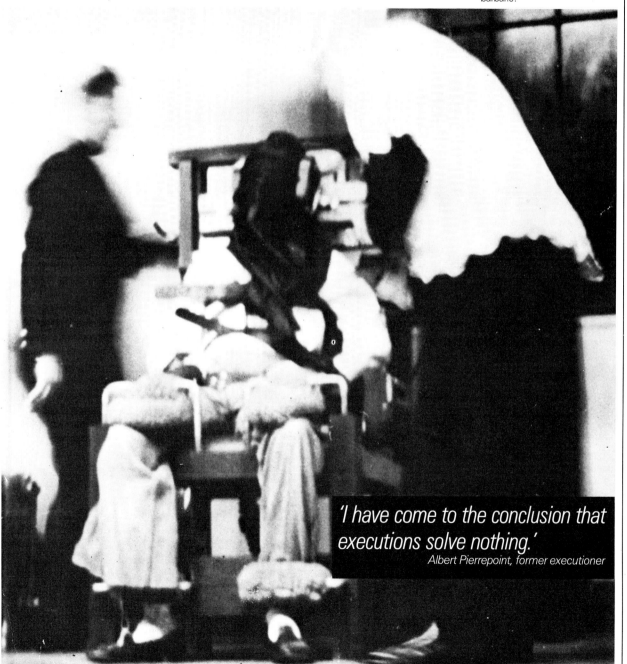

'I have come to the conclusion that executions solve nothing.'

Albert Pierrepoint, former executioner

Reference

Glossary

Appeal – A legal case transferred to a higher court in an effort to change or reverse a previous decision.

Arbitration – The settlement of a dispute by a third, independent party.

Bail – Money against which a person held for trial is temporarily released.

Barrister – A lawyer who argues his client's case in court.

Civil law – The branch of law regulating the rights and duties of individuals in society but excluding matters of crime.

Common law – Unwritten body of law based on usage and tradition.

Criminal law – The branch of law which deals with damaging acts committed against society or individuals.

Defamation – The civil offence of damaging someone's good name or reputation without just cause. *Libel* is written or broadcast defamation. *Slander* is generally spoken.

Habeas corpus – Latin for 'you have the body'. This is a writ issued to bring a person who has been detained before a court and to force the detaining authorities to justify the detention.

Ombudsman – A person who investigates complaints about government, local government or other authorities on behalf of members of the public.

Perjury – The crime of lying or giving false evidence in court under oath.

Solicitor – A lawyer who advises people on legal matters and who represents them in the lower courts.

Subpoena – A court order requiring a person to attend court to give evidence.

Reading list

Alderson, John, *Law and Disorder* (Hamish Hamilton, 1984)
A readable answer to law and order questions from a former chief constable. He argues for closer cooperation between police and public, not for greater severity or increased police power.

Baker, Nigel, *The Law and the Individual* (Macdonald and Evans, 1982)
Clearly sets out the legal framework surrounding the individual.

Berlins, Marcel, and Clare Dyer, *The Law Machine* (Pelican, 1982)
A lively account, based on a TV series, showing how the legal system works.

Boyle, Jimmy, *A Sense of Freedom* (Pan, 1977)
The painful autobiography of a man jailed for murder and struggling to find new ways of understanding. A shocking account of criminal and prison life. Essential reading.

Clarke, R.V.G. and P. Mayhew, *Designing out Crime* (Home Office Research Unit Publications, 1980)
Many interesting ideas on how good design can cut down vandalism and other crimes.

Fitzgerald, Mike, and John Muncie, *System of Justice* (Basil Blackwell, 1983)
An introduction to the criminal justice system of England and Wales which tackles problems as well as describing the system. It covers police and prisons, and the work of the courts. Recommended.

Glover, Jonathan, *Causing Death and Saving Lives* (Pelican, 1977)
Confronts such major problems as abortion and euthanasia within the context of debate about the sanctity of life.

Griffith, J.A.G. *The Politics of the Judiciary* (Fontana, 1977)
This controversial book reveals the narrow background from which British judges are drawn and asks disturbing questions about fairness when political matters are involved.

Lea, J, and J. Young, *What is to be done about Law and Order?* (Penguin, 1984)
An important and powerful book though often difficult. It throws doubt on official crime statistics and sounds a warning against 'military policing'.

Lodge, Juliet (ed.), *Terrorism: a challenge to the state* (Martin Robertson, 1981)
A thought-provoking collection of essays on many different terrorist groups, the particular problems they pose and the response of governments.

Mark, Sir Robert, *Policing a Perplexed Society* (George Allen & Unwin, 1982)
The provocative collected thoughts of an original-minded Metropolitan Police Commissioner. Plenty to agree or disagree with.

Mars, Gerald, *Cheats at Work* (George Allen & Unwin, 1982)
Fascinating anthropological account of fiddling, diddling and general ripping-off at work. Fiddlers are seen as hawks, donkeys, wolves or vultures depending on their style of fiddling. Not always an easy read but certainly interesting.

Mitford, Jessica, *The American Prison Business* (George Allen & Unwin, 1974) (published in the USA as *Kind and Usual Punishment*)
The book that shocked America and then other countries with its account of the injustices and abuse of the US prison system.

Muncie, John, *'The Trouble with Kids Today'* (Hutchinson, 1984)
A sociological work which is bound to increase the self-awareness of young people – if they are prepared to tackle a moderately difficult text. Packed with insights and surprising information. One of the best modern books on youth.

Pearson, Geoffrey, *Hooligan, A History of Respectable Fears* (Macmillan, 1983)
Fascinating account of the way 'law and order' fears have been present in society in something very like their modern form at least since the nineteenth century.

Pierrepoint, Albert, *Executioner: Pierrepoint* (Harrap, 1974)
The macabre autobiography of a man described as 'the world's most famous executioner'. It recounts in detail the hanging of many well-known criminals and how Pierrepoint finally changed his mind about capital punishment.

Scarman, Lord, *The Scarman Report* (HMSO, 1981; and Pelican, 1982)
Report written for the government by a much-respected judge after the Brixton disorders of April 1981. It recommended that police should make greater attempts to consult and understand the community.

Stott, John, and Nick Miller (eds), *Crime and the Responsible Community* (Hodder & Stoughton, 1979)
Essays by figures as diverse as Charles 'Chuck' Colson, President Nixon's adviser who was imprisoned for his part in the Watergate conspiracy, and Sir David McNee, a Metropolitan Police Commissioner. It puts a specifically Christian point of view. Colson's essays are particularly stimulating.

Street, Harry, *Freedom, the Individual and the Law* (Penguin, 1983)
This important book, which has been continuously updated for the past 20 years, has been a watchdog of civil rights and also a powerful agent for changes in the law.

Whittaker, Ben, *The Police in Society* (Sinclair Browne, 1979)
A lengthy but readable book presenting the facts and examining the issues of contemporary policing in an open-minded way.

Wright, Martin, *Making Good: prisons, punishment and beyond* (Burnett Books, 1982)
Another lengthy book but well worth consulting. It argues for fundamental change in our thinking over prisons.

Useful addresses

There are many societies and organizations concerned with different aspects of law and order. Some have produced leaflets and other helpful materials. These are mostly concerned with campaigns for one cause or another. Governments and their agencies will have up-to-date details on legislation.

Penal reform

Howard League for Penal Reform, 322 Kennington Park Rd, London SE11 4PP

John Howard Association, 67 E. Madison St. Sth, 1216 Chicago, Illinois 60603, USA

The John Howard Society of Alberta, Grande Prairie Districts Council, 201, 9917-101 Avenue Grande Prairie, Alberta T8V OX7, Canada

Human rights, torture, and political prisoners

Amnesty International Secretariat, 1 Easton St., London WC1 (for Amnesty addresses in Australia, New Zealand, Canada, India, and around the world)

Amnesty International (British Section), 5 Roberts Place, London, EC1R 0EJ

Abortion

Women's Reproductive Rights Information Centre, 52-4, Featherstone St., London EC1

International Contraception, Abortion and Sterilization Campaign, PO Box 4098, 1009 AB Amsterdam, Holland

Society for the Protection of the Unborn Child, 7 Tufton St., London SW1

Civil rights

National Council for Civil Liberties, 21 Tabard St., London SE1 4LA

Prisoners' rights

National Association for the Care and Resettlement of Offenders, 169 Clapham Rd., London SW9 0PU

Crime prevention

Canadian Association for the Prevention of Crime, 55 Parkdale Avenue, Ottawa, K1A 1E5, Canada

School of Social Science and Welfare Studies, Mitchell College of Advanced Education, Bathurst, NSW 2795, Australia

Euthanasia

Voluntary Euthanasia Society, 13 Prince of Wales Terrace, London W8 5PG

V.E.S. of New South Wales, PO Box 25, Broadway 2007, NSW, Australia

Dying with Dignity, PO Box 232, Station Z, Toronto M5N 223, Canada

The Voluntary Euthanasia Society, 95 Melrose Rd., Island Bay, Wellington 2, New Zealand

Society for the Right to Die with Dignity, 4th Floor, Maneckjee Wadia Building, 127 Mahatma Gandhi Rd., Fort, Bombay 400-001, India

Police procedure

New Scotland Yard, Whitehall, London SW1

Index

The numbers in **bold** refer to illustrations and captions

Credits

The author and publishers
would like to thank the
following for their kind
permission to reproduce
copyright illustrations:

Barnaby's: 10, 26, 50-51
Camera Press: 6, 19, 35, 43, 45,
  46, 54, 59
Mary Evans Picture Library:
  12, 58
Sally & Richard Greenhill: 4-5,
  14, 32, 37, 57
Mike Abrahams/Network: 11,
  23, 53
Katalin Arkell/Network: 56
Judah Passow/Network: 31
John Sturrock/Network: 13, 39
Rex Features: cover
Carlos Reyes: 21, 28, 38, 49
Topham: 7, 9, 15, 16, 17, 25,
  27, 29, 33, 40-41, 42.

Picture research by Diana
  Morris.
Design by Norman Reynolds.